LILLENAS®
DRAMA

I0889931

CHRISTMAS PROGRAM BUILDER

No. 66

Compiled by Heidi Petak

LILLENAS® DRAMA

lillenas®

Questions? Please write or call:
Lillenas Publishing Company
Drama Resources
P. O. Box 419527
Kansas City, MO 64141
Phone: 816-931-1900 • Fax: 816-412-8390
E-mail: drama@lillenas.com
Web Site: www.lillenasdrama.com

Cover Design: Keith Alexander
Executive Editor: Heidi Petak
Supervising Editor: Kimberly Meiste

CONTENTS

Recitations for Preschool

Knock, Knock, Knock! 5
What Can a Baby Do? 5
Little Things 5
Senses 6
The Star 6

Recitations for Ages 6-9

I Like Presents 6
The Things Mary Treasured 7
The Big Gift 7

Recitations and Readings for Ages 10-13

The Best Part of Christmas 8
Treasure Hunt 8

Readings for Teens

Three Wise Guys 9
The Dream 9

Adult Readings

Gladdest Noel 10

Reader's Theater

Peace on Earth 12

Short Sketches

Three-fifths Bank of Mistrust 13
Christmas Plans 17
Where's Your Jesus? 21

One-Act Play

The King's Sword 23

RECITATIONS FOR PRESCHOOL

Knock, Knock, Knock!

Knock, knock, knock *(Children can pretend to knock.)*
At the inn door.
"We're all full.
We can't take anymore!"

Walk, walk, walk *(Children can swing their arms as if walking.)*
Joseph and Mary talk,
"Where will we stay for the night?"

Knock, knock knock *(Children can pretend to knock.)*
At the inn door.
"We're all full.
We can't take anymore!"

Help, help, help! *(Children put their hands against their cheeks.)*
Joseph and Mary say,
"The baby is coming.
And he's coming today!"

Knock, knock, knock *(Children can pretend to knock.)*
At the inn door.
"You can have the stable
And sleep on the floor."

Shhh, shhh, shhh! *(Children can hold one finger in front of their lips)*
The baby is born!
Joy, joy, joy *(Children can wave their arms up in the air.)*
It's the first
Christmas morn!

Beth Swale

What Can a Baby Do?

Can a baby paint a picture?
Can a baby throw a ball?
Babies are so little,
They can't do much at all!

Can a baby put his shoes on?
Can a baby zip his coat?
Can a baby hop on one foot?
Or drink a root beer float?

Jesus was a baby.
He is also King of Kings!
And when He came to earth,
Shepherds heard the angels sing.

He came to give God glory.
He came to die for sin.
He came to bring God's Kingdom,
And sinful hearts to win!

Yes, babies are so tiny
And they can't do many things.
Except for Baby Jesus—
Our Awesome King of Kings!

Beth Swale

Little Things

Little things are little
But they are big things too
'Cause God might have a big, big job
For little things to do!

Noelle Nelson

Senses

Feel the hay
Scratchy, scratchy

Smell the pig
Stinky, stinky

Hear the cow
Mooing, mooing

Touch the sheep
Wooly, wooly

See the manger
Softly, softly

Hold the baby
Sleeping, sleeping
April Kelly

The Star

Reach up high! *(they stand on their toes and reach up high with their hands)*
Touch the sky!
I see a star!
It's not very far!

I'm gonna get it!
I got it! *(they pretend to grab the star out of the sky and bring it down to look at it in their hands)*

This one is so bright!
It shines in the night!
And shouts loud and clear
That Jesus is here! *(they gasp)*
Uh- oh!

The wise men need to know
They need to know where to go!
I'd better put it back
Before somebody loses track!

In the sky, but where?
Yes! Over the stable, there!
(they pretend to put the star back in the sky)

Shine light, shine bright!
Baby Jesus is born tonight!
Noelle Nelson

RECITATIONS FOR AGES 6 TO 9

I Like Presents

I like presents
They're just my style
They make me happy
At least for a while

But then I'm bored
And need something new
Shiny and red
Or amazing and blue

The only present
That brings lasting joy
Is the Bethlehem birth
Of a baby boy
Bruce Hoeker

The Things Mary Treasured

First came an angel saying, "Don't
  be afraid!"
Then came the news of God's Son.
Next was the manger where the
  baby was laid.
Then came the shepherds, one by
  one.

An angel song, a star in the sky,
She rocked her new baby with love.
The cows and the sheep and the
  donkey stood by
Watching God's gift from above.

And then came the kings, who
  traveled so far,
Their camels with treasure-filled
  packs.
They came to the manger, led by the
  star,
Then climbed off the tall camel's
  backs.

The kings knelt down before her son
She didn't know what to say!
They gave him gifts, one by one
While the baby just slept on the hay.

She treasured these things deep
  down in her heart
Amazed to be part of the story.
God planned to save the world from
  the start,
And do it all for His glory!

Beth Swale

The Big Gift

I've been dreaming of a present
A great big one with a bow
Sitting underneath the tree
Where branches hang down low

I don't want something little
Like some scissors or some glue
I want something really big
Like a bike that's red and blue
(pretends to receive a little gift box)

Oh, wait, what is this?
It's little, don't you know?
  (sighs)
I don't want something little
And besides, where's the bow?
*(pretends to open the top of the box
  and take something out- as if
  four letters are hanging from a
  ribbon)*

Look! It's four letters!
L-O-V-E!
God sent his love to earth
As a little gift, a baby!

Oh! Now this IS big
It's not little like I thought
If God gave us His love
Then He must love us all a lot!

Lauren West

RECITATIONS AND READINGS FOR AGES 10 TO 13

The Best Part of Christmas

The best part of Christmas is candy
Like chocolate, so gooey and sweet
I'll take some more if you've got it
Candy for me, can't be beat

The best part of Christmas is reindeer
I've been watching the window all night
Mom says they won't come till I'm sleeping
That doesn't seem fair, am I right?

The best part of Christmas is in-laws
Mommy said with a smile, I think
Then she looked at my dad with a nod
And he looked back at her with a wink

The best part of Christmas is snow
I could play out in it all day
I'm cold and I'm frozen straight through
But I'd still stay out if I may

But the very best part of Christmas is Jesus
When we celebrate His holy birth
Because He is the reason for Christmas
That God's love has come down to earth.

Bruce Hoeker

Treasure Hunt

I was looking for treasure
Shiny and bold
I was looking for treasure
Silver and gold

I followed a star
And hoped that it led
To jewels and money
All for me, I said

But when I arrived
I peeked in the door
And saw Mary and Joseph
And hay on the floor

I thought I'd been had
Where's the treasure? I thought.
I came all this way
This is all that I got?
It was then that I saw him
The baby so small
And I realized I'd found
The best treasure of all

David O'Brien

READINGS FOR TEENS

Three Wise Guys

For Three Readers

1: Three wise guys
2: A.K.A. Magis
3: Used their eyes
2: To search the skies
1: Not for French fries
3: Or apple pies
1: But for a prize
2: In the skies
3: A star.
ALL: Surprise!
2: They theorized
1: And asked their why's
3: With no replies
1: So the three did rise
2: And packed supplies
3: Said their goodbyes
2: To their wives
3: Traveled lows and highs
1: Under the moonrise
2: Searched like spies
1: And followed the prize
3: With their wise eyes
2: Stopped at a low rise
1: Not a high rise
2: And found the pint-sized true prize
ALL: A baby's cries!
1: The worshipping Magis
3: Gave gifts of great size
2: Then fearing Jesus' demise
3: From an angel's advice
2: They said their goodbyes
1: And did devise
3: A route revise
1: And went home to their wives.
2: So when we have why's
3: With no replies
2: Let's look to the skies
1: And fix our eyes
2: On Jesus the prize
ALL: Like those three wise guys.

Heidi Petak

The Dream

I had a dream that people were fighting
Hitting
Splitting
Smashing my life to pieces
My life

No one could put it together again

Not the kings' horses
Not the kings' men

I had a dream that people were fighting
Abusing
Accusing
Smashing my heart to pieces
My heart

No one could put it together again

Not the king's horses
Not the king's men

(pause)

The Dream, *continued*

But…what about the King?
Could the king do better than his
horses or men?
(tone becomes hopeful)

I had a dream the King was coming
Caring
Daring
He picked up the pieces of my life
My heart
Breathed His power of redemption
And made them new
Made me new
New life
New heart.

Wonderful Counselor, Mighty God,
Everlasting Father, Prince of
Peace.

Lauren West

ADULT READING

Gladdest Noel

by J. Bernadette Williamson

In a lowly lonely corner
Of a dark and dismal earth
What man once lost
Was found again
Hope was given birth

Calamitous our condition:
Under judgment from The Fall
Till the gladdest, brightest miracle
Came down to save us all

He heard us crying in the night
Dying in our sins
So in unblemished love
God slipped into our common skin

And The Word became flesh
And the greatest became least
And swaddling clothes were
wrapped around
Heaven's Highest Priest

(In) Teeny tiny fingers
And teeny tiny toes
Baby soft and sweet to kiss
Lay Sharon's tender Rose

Desire of All Nations
Spreading His rich perfume
As morning sheds her glory
Across the shimmering dew

Oh holy night
God of virgin born
Prophecy fulfilled
Fathomless, alone

But the serpent of Eden
Hissed heinously and groaned
For the Savior had returned
To claim back His rightful own

The snake he slid and slithered
In reviling rant and rave
For men's life was not his purpose
He was hell-bent on their grave

So be'sniveling from the manger
In green-eyed insanity

He crawled off to hew a rugged cross
From just the perfect tree

In search surpassing sinister
Yet sovereignly allowed
He also plucked the perfect thorns
For Rose of Sharon's brow

And in these things
He had his way
But only till the stain
Of Jesus blood had washed away our sins
Till none remained.

And the wrath of God was violent
And the terror cruel and raw
Not at all the thing we want to see
When looking in the straw

At an infant pure and innocent
But we must reconcile
With this truth: The price to set men free
Was held within this child

The Lion of Judah
Who died for us our death
Whose throne can be our very hearts
Whose breath
Can be our breath (Our very breath!)

Whose Life can be our life
For all eternity
If we will but accept the gift
He sent for you and me

Jesus is His name
Noel Noel
Messiah-Deliverer
Emanuel
Holy One of Israel
The Prince of Peace
Almighty-Counselor
Our Sinless High Priest

God of all gods
Light of all lights
Joy in our sorrow
Rest in our nights
Blessed Redeemer
Bright Morning Star
Wonder of wonders
What a wonder You are!

Comforter-Helper
Faithful Friend
Promise Keeper
Of Bethlehem
King of all Kings
Lord of all Lords
Ancient of Days
Forevermore

Immortal Invisible
Merciful One
Forgiver
Of every vile thing we have done
Righteous-Victorious
Our All in All
And yet His eye sees
When a wee sparrow falls

And when we are weak
He is strong
And when we are wandering
His arms are long
And when pain runs deep
His love's deeper still
If we will but ask Him
He'll save us He will

Beautiful Savior
Bethlehem's Bloom
Hope for the tiniest
Forms within wombs
Loving kind Rescuer
Of helpless man
No one can steal us
Out of Your (His) hands

Noel Noel
Gladdest Noel
Jesus is born
All is well.

READER'S THEATER

Peace on Earth

by Amy Green

(At rise, READERS 1-5 *stand in front of the audience, spaced out along the sage. They may read their lines from a book or have them memorized.)*

READER 1: It's one of the holiday season's most popular phrases.

READER 3: You can find it written in Christmas cards ...

READER 5: ... sung on the radio ....

READER 2: ... and, ironically, printed all over sigsn at the mall during the stressful holiday shopping rush.

READER 4: Christians or atheists, young or old, rich or poor—it doesn't seem to matter. Everyone seems to believe in this simple creed.

READER 3: Or, at least, they all want to believe in it.

ALL: Peace on earth.

READER 2: The angels announced it in Bethlehem more than two thousand years ago, in a mighty, resounding proclamation.

READER 3: And there have been echoes ever since.

READER 4 *(after slight pause):* But they seem to be getting fainter.

READER 1: If the angels were right, where is the peace on earth today? It seems like we have nothing but turmoil.

READER 2: War.

READER 3: Broken families.

READER 4: Disasters.

READER 5: Suffering.

READER 3: Our earth needs peace.

READER 2: Our families need peace.

READER 1: Our hearsts need peace.

READER 5: Maybe the angels weren't only proclaiming good news to the shepherds.

READER 4: Maybe they were proclaiming good news to us.

READER 1: Jesus, the Messiah, was called manythings in the Bible.

READER 5: The Lamb of God, who died to pay for our sins.

READER 2: The Light of the World, bringing truth into the darkness.

READER 4: Emmanuel, which means "God With Us."

READER 3: *And* ... a shepherd.

READER 1 *(Reading from scroll):* He will stand and shepherd his flock int he strength of the Lord ...

ALL: And he will be their peace.

READER 5: Our circumstances might not change. We will still have hardships, stress, grief, and suffering.

READER 1: But Jesus came to give us the most important kind of lpeace: peace with God. He died on the cross to take the punsihment we deserve.

READER 4: If we accept his gift of salvation, we have something the rest of the world can't ver truly understand, even at Christmas: hope.

READER 2: No matter what.

READER 3: And that's what the angels were talking about that first Christmas night. Hope through Jesus ... and peace on Earth.

(Readers return to their seats.)

SHORT SKETCHES

Three-fifths Bank of Mistrust

Cast of Characters:

VP OF LENDING, Mr. Filthy Lucre

SECRETARY, Ms. Anna Helper

MR. HANSEL ADAMS

MRS. GRETEL ADAMS

(Setting is lobby & VP office of 3/5 Bank of Mistrust. SECRETARY *and* VP *are both working at their desks.* MR. & MRS. ADAMS *enter bank.)*

GRETEL: Well, here we are. I'm just not so sure I want to go through with it.

HANSEL: There's no other choice dear. The family is depending on us.

GRETEL: There must be another way.

HANSEL: I don't think so. They've come to expect big, expensive gifts. We have no choice.

SECRETARY: Hello, how may I help you today?

Hansel: We have an appointment with Mr. Lucre.

SECRETARY: *(Checks calendar on desk)* Sure, you must be Mr. & Mrs. Adams. Come right on in.

(Leads them back to Mr. Filthy Lucre's office.)

SECRETARY: Mr. Lucre, Mr. & Mrs. Adams are here.

MR. LUCRE: *(Extends his right hand to shake with the Adams)* Yes, you are right on time. I'm reviewing your file now.

HANSEL: *(Notices a big stack of papers)* That's not our file is it?

MR. LUCRE: As a matter of fact, it is. We in the banking business like to keep our eye on the past as past behavior is a good predictor of future behavior. Do you realize through our collection of highly sophisticated electronic databases, we can track your every financial move? For instance, these reports tell me that you were late on your telephone bill back in 2002 by two days.

GRETEL: You know about that?

MR. LUCRE: That and much more. *(flips through pages)* Looks like you were late on a Visa payment by one week, JCPenney by 3 days, Sears you were late a few times and you missed paying your electric bill on time by fifty-seven minutes ten years ago. Oh yes, we know all about your little financial sins. Nothing is hidden or forgotten might I add.

HANSEL: But, I thought we had a good credit score?

MR. LUCRE: Ah yes, the SICO score. *(Calls out to secretary)* Ms. Helper, please bring in the Adams SICO score reports.

SECRETARY: *(Enters and drops another large stack of paperwork on the desk.)* Here you are Mr. Lucre.

MR. LUCRE: Mr. Adams it appears your score is 795 and Mrs. Adams' is 798.

HANSEL: Isn't that good? I thought the top was 800.

MR. LUCRE: Well, the top is 800 but we look at more than the SICO score here at 3/5 Bank of Mistrust. You see, Mr. & Mrs. Adams, we are quite particular about the kind of people we do business with. We don't accept everyone.

GRETEL: Well, what are you saying?

MR. LUCRE: I am saying that we do not accept everyone who will apply for a loan. Your good works will not guarantee a loan here at 3/5 Bank of Mistrust. (Smiles) However, in your case, I think we can work something out.

HANSEL: It's been a while since we needed to borrow some money. The last loan we had was an auto loan for a brand new Chevrolet, top-of-the-line, back in 1993.

MR. LUCRE: *(Looks through file)* Yes, I see that a candy apple red Impala. A nice car, I'll bet…for the day.

HANSEL: Oh, it sure was. Anyway, we paid that loan off in 48 months and was never late on a payment.

MR. LUCRE: Actually, you were late one time.

GRETEL: Surely, one late payment on a loan so long ago won't stop us from getting a loan this time will it?

MR. LUCRE: I'm inclined to give you a second chance. However, that puts you in our high risk category.

GRETEL: High risk, for one late payment twenty years ago?

MR. LUCRE: Not just one late car payment twenty years ago. There are some other infractions as we discussed before. Remember the financial sins I mentioned?

HANSEL: I'm not sure they should be called sins but since when does the bank care about somebody being a couple of days late on a phone bill?

MR. LUCRE: We can't take financial matters lightly. We're kind of like the church. I am sure your church doesn't take spiritual matters lightly, now does it?

HANSEL: Well, no but..

GRETEL: But when the Lord forgives, he forgets. He doesn't keep bringing up old sins time and time again. This bank certainly doesn't operate like God or the church.

MR. LUCRE: Now, Mrs. Adams. No need to get anxious. I have decided to grant your loan.

HANSEL: That's great news!

GRETEL: Actually, I think we've changed our minds.

MR. LUCRE: *(Angrily)* You can't change your mind. *(Softens)* I mean…you don't want to do that. I've already completed the paperwork. Let's review it now. You need this money, Mrs. Adams. Your family is depending on it. You said so yourself. See here on your application? *(Shoves it toward her.)*

HANSEL: Hon, he's right. I think we need the loan.

MR. LUCRE: Smart man. Okay, here we go. The law requires I give nearly full disclosure of the fees involved. Just follow along now, this is rather tedious, *(begins pointing to line items on the page in front of them)* here is the application fee, loan processing fee, underwriting fee, bank examiner fee, execution fee, security fee, negotiation with lender fee, pledge agreement fee, loan validity fee, customer liability fee, document transfer fee, borrower notification fee, interest and penalties…

GRETEL: Wait a minute, penalties…for what?

MR. LUCRE: Anticipated penalties Mrs. Adams. The APR/GFE/DUM law requires that because of your past financial sins we anticipate penalties. It's standard practice I assure you. Anyway, for your loan of $2,000; your final payment will be due in the year 2099 and total amount paid including finance charges will be in the neighborhood of $38,223.10.

GRETEL: *(Shocked)* You've got to be kidding me!

HANSEL: Mr. Lucre, that's a lot more than we anticipated. What was the interest rate? Maybe you could explain those fees again.

GRETEL: That won't be necessary. *(Turns to her husband)* Hansel, this is crazy. Christmas is not about how much we spend or what we buy for our family. I think they'll understand that. Christmas is about celebrating the gift God gave us, His Son. We don't need a loan and a true Christmas can't be bought anyway.

MR. LUCRE: But wait…the 3/5 Bank of Mistrust wants to help you celebrate the Christ child. We support the religious community and I assure you, you can buy a beautiful Christmas. If you're concerned about the little financial sins we talked about, perhaps, I can look the other way and reduce the interest rate a bit.

HANSEL: No, Mr. Lucre, thank you. But my wife is right. We're not looking for someone to support the religious community by leading folks to believe they can buy Christmas. Thank you for your time but we'll be on our way now. *(Hansel & Gretel get up to leave.)*

GRETEL: And let me assure you Mr. Lucre, when God forgives a sin, it is forgotten. It is as far as the east is from the west. He won't bring it up again in 20 years. Let's go Hansel.

(Hansel and Gretel stand up and begin walking toward the door.)

MR. LUCRE: *(Calling after the Adams)* Can I interest you in a New Year's loan? Why not start the year right with money in your hands and your pockets to do what you want to right from the start? I assure you, we've got the lowest introductory rate for the first 30 days of anywhere in town……

THE END

Christmas Plans

by Heidi Petak

CHARACTERS

- Harold
- Margie

PROPS

two recliners or chairs	tea cup	Avalon CD
end table	Santa costume	stereo
bell	Christmas tree with lights	plate of fudge
phone	clock	Bible

SOUND EFFECTS

Sound of a car stopping, car door slamming, Avalon song, phone ringing

HAROLD *sits in his recliner or chair, napping with his eyes closed. He's dressed in a Santa coat and pants.* MARGIE *is sitting in her recliner or chair near him, engrossed in the end of a Christmas movie.*

MARGIE *(along with the television):* ... an angel gets its wings! Oh, Harold, is that not the sweetest thing? (*she takes a bell from the end table and rings it*). I'm making another angel get its wings…right now! (*she rings it again*) Harold! Are you sleeping?

HAROLD *(he opens his eyes wide):* Yes! I mean, no! No, Margie, I was just resting.

MARGIE: Resting. So tell me what the movie was about.

HAROLD: Christmas. It was about Christmas.

MARGIE *(sighs, rising from her chair):* You're getting old.

HAROLD: And somehow I married a woman who grows younger with each sunrise. All right, tell me the movie was not about Christmas.

MARGIE: It was.

HAROLD: Well then?

MARGIE *(chuckling):* I'm going to make some cinnamon tea. Would you like a cup? *(exits during his answer)*

HAROLD: No. I'll have some hot chocolate with Chris and Kelly and the kids when they get here. What time is it?

MARGIE *(offstage):* Nearly eight.

HAROLD: Ooh, I'd better get ready. *(he begins to put on his Santa hat and beard)* They will be here any minute. *(he sings a line or two from a Christmas carol while he gets ready, then calls to Margie)* Whaddaya bet Tyler is a foot taller now. Probably likes girls already. I can't wait to give him a grizzly bear hug!

MARGIE *(offstage):* Kelly said Madeline is bringing her ballet outfit from her recital so she can do her dance for us. Isn't that sweet?

HAROLD: Sweet as sugar. *(goes back to singing his Christmas carol, imitates a crooner.* MARGIE *joins him from offstage. Suddenly the lights go out on the Christmas tree.)*

HAROLD: Well, what in sam hill? Margie, are you playing around with the electricity in there?

MARGIE: No dear. *(from offstage)* Unless you call checking on the fudge playing around. (*she comes out with her cup of tea*)

HAROLD *(going over to the tree):* Don't tell me we've got a bulb out.

MARGIE: I won't.

HAROLD: Unless we do.

MARGIE: We might have a bulb out.

HAROLD: Be an optimist, Margie! Maybe they'll just come back on. *(they stand together looking at the tree)* Of course, if we sit here looking at them they'll never come back on.

MARGIE: A watched pot never boils.

HAROLD: So let's turn around. *(they turn around with their backs to the tree for five seconds, and then turn back around)* Nope. Better start checking the bulbs. One of 'em's loose, I know it; we just gotta find it. *(they start checking bulbs together; the sound of a car is heard outside)*

MARGIE: That could be them. *(she goes to the window. Looks out.* HAROLD *adjusts his beard)* Nope. Must be Louise's sister. She said she'd have a visitor this year. I keep praying those two little boys next door will have a visitor this year, too.

HAROLD *(still checking bulbs):* Fat chance of that happening.

MARGIE: Be an optimist, Harold. Their father just might come home. You never know.

HAROLD: And these lights just might come back on. You never know. (*beat*) How's that fudge comin'?

MARGIE: Absolutely perfect. *(going back into the kitchen)* I think it's ready. Want a piece?

HAROLD: Do reindeer fly?

MARGIE *(from offstage):* I think this time of year they do.

HAROLD: We need to put on a Christmas record. *(going over to the stereo, calling* MARGIE*)* What record do ya wanna hear?

MARGIE *(coming back in with a piece of fudge):* Let's hear that new one. The young kids. You know, that group that's the same as the Toyota.

HAROLD: You mean Avalon? (*he finds it, puts it on the cd player*)

MARGIE: They have got some soul. *(the music starts.* HAROLD *takes a bite of his fudge, then starts to dance, sweeping* MARGIE *with him. After a few moments, the phone rings.* MARGIE *goes to get it, while* HAROLD *keeps dancing, relishing the fudge.* MARGIE *answers and talks long enough to hear the news, asks a few questions, looks disappointed, then hangs up)* Harold! Harold! (*He can't hear her, and he's still dancing. She goes to the CD player and turns the music off*)

HAROLD: Well whadja do that for?

MARGIE: Because Chris and Kelly and the kids aren't coming.

HAROLD: You mean they're going to be late?

MARGIE: No, I mean they're not coming.

HAROLD: Not tonight, but they're coming tomorrow?

MARGIE: Kelly's mother just went to the hospital with severe chest pain. They're turning around to go back home.

HAROLD: I've had severe chest pain before and it was gas, remember?

MARGIE: The doctor told Kelly to get there as soon as they can.

HAROLD: So they're not coming?

MARGIE: No.

HAROLD: I won't be giving Tyler a grizzly bear hug?

MARGIE: No, honey. And we won't see Madeline dance. I'm disappointed, too.

*(*HAROLD *sits down in his recliner, takes off his hat.* MARGIE *sits down in her chair. They are quiet for a moment.)*

MARGIE: Want another piece of fudge?

HAROLD: No.

MARGIE: Some hot chocolate?

HAROLD: No. (*beat*) Wanna hear any more Toyota?

MARGIE: No.

HAROLD *(sighs, rises):* Well, guess we might as well go to bed. *(he starts taking off his beard).*

MARGIE *(rising):* I guess so. *(looking at the clock)* Harold, it's only eight o'clock.

HAROLD *(crossing to exit):* What else is there to do?

MARGIE: We could play scrabble?

HAROLD: Nah.

MARGIE: Harold. Look at us.

HAROLD: What?

MARGIE: We're acting like Christmas is ruined.

HAROLD: It is!

MARGIE *(rises, crosses to him):* I seem to remember someone telling me to be an optimist a few minutes ago.

HAROLD: Was that me?

MARGIE: That was you.

HAROLD: I know. It's just that I've been looking forward to this for months.

MARGIE: We both have.

HAROLD: I was going to read the kids the Christmas story tonight. I rehearsed my angel voice and everything. "Do not be afraid. I bring you good news of great joy that will be for all people. You will find a baby wrapped in swaddling clothes and lying in a manger."

MARGIE: Very nice. And I think I like the idea of Santa reading the Christmas story. *(she gets an idea)* Honey! You could read it to **me**.

HAROLD: Thank you, but you're not quite the audience of a 5 and a 7 year old. *(he gets an idea)* Wait a minute. You don't think...? No. Probably not.

MARGIE: What?

HAROLD: Nothing. Let's go to bed. *(he goes back to get his Santa hat off the floor by the chair)*

MARGIE: You can't do that, Harold! You can't leave me on pins and needles wondering what you're thinking.

HAROLD: Well, you were saying some little boys next door might be hoping for a visitor. *(he fingers his hat and looks at the floor)*

MARGIE: Yes...

HAROLD: You don't suppose they would like a couple old folks visiting, do you?

MARGIE: I think they might! Especially since one of those old folks is dressed like Santa.

HAROLD: The other old folk could bring some fudge...

MARGIE: Yes, she could. I'll go get it! *(exits to kitchen)*

HAROLD *(picking up the Bible off the end table, he practices):* "Do not be afraid! I bring you good news of great joy that shall be for all people."

MARGIE *(re-enters with her dish of fudge):* Ready?

HAROLD: Wait. *(he puts on his beard. Their backs are to the Christmas tree. Suddenly, the lights turn back on. They don't see them.)* Now I'm ready. *(they sing as they exit)*

TOGETHER *(singing):* O come all ye faithful, joyful and triumphant...

Stage lights fade, while Christmas tree lights remain on.

END

Where's Your Jesus?

by Gary D. Canfield

Running Time: 3 minutes

Theme: What do you do with Jesus after the holidays?

Suggested use: Worship service during the Christmas holidays

Cast:

MAN
CHILD

Props:

Cell phone
Red wagon

(MAN enters talking on cell phone. He needs to pause between sentences like he is having a conversation with someone on the other line. He is a bit frantic and impatient.)

MAN: Hello, pastor. *(Pause)* I am fine. How are you? Well, actually, I'm not fine. We've got a problem, a big problem. Someone has stolen Jesus. *(Pause)* Jesus, you know . . . Jesus, God's son. *(Pause)* I know you know who Jesus is, but someone has stolen Him. He's no longer here. At the nativity—someone stole Jesus from our nativity scene right out in front of the church. *(Pause)* No, I'm not kidding! *(Pause)* Well, yeah, I am standing right here. There is no Jesus. *(Pause)* Now why would anyone need to borrow Jesus. Doesn't that seem a little strange to you? *(Pause)* I don't know for sure how long He's been gone. I know for certain He was here yesterday. *(Pause)* Well, because on Christmas day we always take a fruitcake to Mrs. Morris' house across the street from the church. *(Pause)* Well, no, I didn't know she didn't like fruitcake. *(Pause)* She's allergic to nuts? She never told us that. I wonder why. She always seemed so happy to get it. *(Pause)* Huh, yeah, I'll be here. I'll just wait on you. OK, goodbye.

(Talking to himself) She doesn't like fruitcake. Boy, is that a kick in the head! Why did she never tell us? She just kept pretending she liked it? Can't say I blame her, that's the nastiest stuff every created. Who in the world likes fruitcake anyway?

(As he continues to talk to himself, a CHILD pulling a brand new red wagon with a baby doll wrapped in a blanket comes walking by. MAN looks and notices the wagon.)

MAN: Hey, little man, where are you heading?

CHILD: Oh, nowhere in particular, mister. Just walking.

MAN *(notices baby in wagon)*: Who do you have in your little red wagon? *(Pauses and says suspiciously)* Hey, where did you get that baby? Did you steal it from our manger scene?

CHILD: No mister, I didn't steal it!

MAN: Well it sure does look like our baby Jesus; is that from our manger scene?

CHILD: Yup. But I didn't steal it. I borrowed it.

MAN: Borrowed it? *(Irritated)* You borrowed it from our church. What were you thinking? You can't just borrow it. You stole it, didn't you? Come on, admit it: you stole Jesus.

CHILD: Nope! I didn't steal it. I just borrowed it.

MAN: Where do you live, young man? I need to have a word with your parents, and I might just call the police.

CHILD: I didn't steal it. I'm just giving Jesus a ride.

MAN: A ride? Now, why would baby Jesus want a ride in a red wagon?

CHILD: Because I told Him that if He would make sure I got a new little red wagon for Christmas, He'd be the first one to ride in it. So I gave Him a ride around the block.

MAN *(humbled):* Around the block, huh? *(Pause)* Well, I'm glad you kept your promise. Come on. Let me help you put the baby back in the manger. *(Take doll out of wagon)*

CHILD: I think He liked it better in my wagon.

MAN: Probably so, but this doll represents Jesus every Christmas, so He has to stay in the manger.

CHILD: So, what do you do with Him after Christmas?

MAN: Well, we pack Him away in a box with all the other Christmas decorations.

CHILD: You pack Jesus away in a box like another decoration? Why?

MAN: Well, I . . . why? *(Stammering)* I guess I don't know.

CHILD: If I were you, I'd want Jesus around all year long.

MAN: You have a good point, son. I'll ah . . . I'll have to ask the pastor what we can do about that.

CHILD: OK. Bye. *(Exits with empty wagon)*

MAN: Bye. *(Calling)* Hi, pastor. Baby Jesus has been found. *(Pause)* Well, actually, He was never lost. Pastor, do you think it might be disrespectful to pack baby Jesus away in a box after Christmas? *(Pause)* Right. But I just met a little boy who got me thinking: there is one thing at Christmas that should make a difference in our lives the rest of the year, too. *(Pause)* No sir, I was not thinking of fruitcake. Not fruitcake. Just Jesus. *(Begins to exit talking on phone)* But Jesus, we've gotta make sure we don't ever pack the real Jesus away in a box of Christmas decorations. Yeah, that would definitely be . . . *(Exits completely)*

ONE-ACT PLAY

The King's Sword

by Goerky Smith

Running Time: 1 hour

Synopsis: A child dreams of serving in the King's army

Cast:

PETER—A young boy of 11 to 13 years of age

MARIAN—Peter's oldest sister, 14 to 18 years of age

DEBORAH—Peter's sister, 8 to 11 years of age

TABITHA—Peter's 4 or 5 year-old sister

JAMES—Peter's younger brother, 3 or 4 years of age

NAOMI—Deborah's friend

DORCAS—Deborah's friend

PRISCILLA—Deborah's friend

BOYS—Students in the synagogue class

GIRLS—Girls in Marian's home study class

MARK—Peter's friend

TIMOTHY—Peter's friend

CHILDREN

JESUS—A child between 1 and 2 years of age

MARY

Joseph

SCENE 1

(Lights up on a humble home made of rubble stone. An US door, wooden or curtained with rough burlap fabric, opens to the outside. SR of the door is a window. DCS a low, rough-hewn table holds a large clay pot, three small bowls, and a basket of rolls. A bench or shelf with baskets and jars is on the left wall. As the lights come up, DEBORAH *stirs the pot with a wooden spoon.* JAMES *and* TABITHA *play on the floor pretending to cook with small clay pots and sticks for spoons.)*

TABITHA *(gets up to look in the stew pot):* That doesn't look nutritional, Deborah.

DEBORAH: Tabitha, the breakfast menu is stewed figs. Period. End of discussion.

JAMES *(looks in the bowl):* Not nutritional.

TABITHA *(pouting):* This makes me not hungry.

JAMES: Not hungry! *(Grabs a roll when* DEBORAH *isn't watching, turns his back to her and stuffs it in his mouth.)*

DEBORAH *(cajoling):* Aunt Lydia has gone to the market to get meat for stew, Tabitha. And, we'll have a treat tonight because Marian is coming home for the holidays! Please eat.

TABITHA: Marian's coming home? Now? *(Runs to the window and stands on her toes, trying to look out)* Is Marian home now?

DEBORAH *(irritated):* James—Tabitha—sit down and eat!

TABITHA: I hear Uncle John's donkey in the driveway.

DEBORAH: No, you don't. I said, sit down!

TABITHA *(whining):* I want Marian. You're too grumpy.

JAMES *(sits at table):* Marian's a good cook. *(Stares at bowl, but doesn't eat.)*

DEBORAH *(slams ladle down):* Who cares. Nobody loves me. I don't care if you eat cobblestones!

JAMES: May I please have cobblestones?

TABITHA: That's good, Deb. I don't want figs. I'll take the cobblestones!

*(*DEBORAH *crosses to DL, sits with her knees pulled up to her chest, and her chin propped on her fists.* JAMES *and* TABITHA *begin to cry.)*

PRISCILLA *(outside):* Deborah? It's me, Priscilla. Are you here?

*(*PRISCILLA *enters, followed by* NAOMI *and* DORCAS. JAMES *and* TABITHA *stop whining.* DEBORAH *hastily rubs a tear with the back of her fist and greets her visitors.* TABITHA, *excited for the diversion, greets the girls who hug her.)*

NAOMI: I am so hungry! What's cooking? *(Looks in bowl and sniffs)* Stewed figs! Gross me back to the Garden of Eden.

DORCAS: Hi, Deb. We came to see your sister Marian. Is she back yet?

PRISCILLA: Isn't it exciting. Having a sister who lives in a king's palace.

NAOMI: And look at how you dress, Deb. *(Giggles and holds hand to mouth)* Doesn't she ever give you any of her old clothes?

DORCAS: See what I got from Hanukkah? *(Spins around, pulling a scarf across her face like an Arab princess)* I'll have more pretty things this week. Father traded goods with a caravan of foreigners. Rich foreigners! He met them while he was at market in Jerusalem. They gave him beautiful gifts for answering some silly questions.

PRISCILLA: Was it a camel caravan? My brother said that rich strangers came into Bethlehem today asking questions about a new King.

NAOMI: A new King? As if we don't have enough trouble with the old one. King Herod the Not-so-Great.

*(*NAOMI *clasps* TABITHA *and* JAMES' *hands, and they dance in a circle chanting "Horrid old King Herod" several times. The other girls are horrified. Finally,* PRISCILLA *grabs* NAOMI *and shakes her.)*

PRISCILLA: Stop it, Naomi. Stop it! If a Roman soldier heard you, we would be killed.

NAOMI: Kill a child? You think a soldier would kill a child? You're too serious, Priscilla. You're no fun at all.

PRISCILLA: Don't you listen to the news? One of the first things he did when he got to be king was to kill millions of—

NAOMI: Millions is not the same as dozens, Priscilla.

PRISCILLA: Fine. Dozens. He killed dozens of religious leaders, then he killed his own wife. We're nothing. He would swat us like . . . like garbage.

NAOMI *(rolls eyes):* That's a mixed metaphor. He would swat us like *flies.*

PRISCILLA: I don't care about your old metaphors. Dead is still dead.

NAOMI: Well, ex-cu-se me! I have to go now. I only wanted to see if Marian was home.

DORCAS: Bye, Deborah. Tell Marian about my new scarf.

PRISCILLA *(hugs* JAMES *and* TABITHA*):* Bye, Deborah.

(After they exit, DEBORAH *sits on the floor again, her chin propped on her hands.* JAMES *and* TABITHA *look at the bowls of food, shake their heads, then take a small roll and sit on the floor. They bow their heads in thanks, then eat.)*

MARIAN *(peeks into the house):* Is anyone home?

JAMES/TABITHA: Marian! Marian! Marian! You're home! We're hungry. We're starving.

*(*TABITHA *and* JAMES *run to greet her, grabbing her hands and talking excitedly.* DEBORAH *ignores* MARIAN, *who doesn't see her.)*

MARIAN: Tabitha, I've missed you. *(Takes two oranges from her pouch or apron and gives them to the* CHILDREN.*)* My, how you've grown, James, in one short month! *(Looks around)* Why, DEBORAH, I didn't see you. How have you been?

DEBORAH *(sarcastic):* I'm sure you didn't see me.

MARIAN: What's wrong?

(Kneels beside DEBORAH *and tries to hand her an orange, which her sister ignores, so she puts it back in her pocket)*

DEBORAH: Nothing. Just nothing.

MARIAN *(sighs):* Little sister, I know you've had a lot on you since I've been gone, but your help is really needed. Where would we have gone, you, me, James, Tabitha, and Peter? I thank God every day for Aunt Lydia and Uncle John. They love us as though we were their own.

DEBORAH *(sadly):* I know.

MARIAN *(hugs her and wipes away her tears):* There now. And for my favorite oldest sister—

*(*MARIAN *hands* DEBORAH *the orange again which is accepted with the beginnings of a smile.)*

MARIAN: Now you look more like my lovely sister. And where is Peter, Deborah?

(On cue, PETER *throws open the door and jumps into the room, brandishing a sword. He soundly whacks the wooden table. The others jump in surprise.* MARIAN *laughs and hugs him, but* DEBORAH *crosses her arms and scowls.)*

PETER *(bows gallantly):* Gentle maid. Welcome to humble Bethlehem. As a spy in the palace of Herod the Horrible in the great city of Jerusalem, what news do you bring? Have there been any more massacres? Assassinations?

MARION *(frowns and holds up a hand to warn him):* Oh Peter, this is not a game. You must be careful! Each day as I clean in the palace, I realize that one mistake—one small mistake—could be my last and put our family in great danger.

PETER *(offended):* It's not a game. When our new King comes I shall be the captain of His guard. We will take the palace, and I—I will challenge Herod to come out and fight like a man. *(He fights across the room to DCS, waving his sword furiously.)* Come out, you Jewish traitor! You Roman dog!

MARIAN *(frightened):* Peter, stop! *(Takes him by the shoulders, then puts a hand over his mouth)* You want news from the city? Hear this: All of Jerusalem is upset because there are kings from the East looking for a new King, a King of the Jews. You know that the evil Herod calls himself our king. He killed his own wife when he thought she might be against him. He would crush us all like bugs if he heard such talk.

PETER *(excited):* You don't have to worry about me, sister! *(Swaggers to DCS, crosses his arms and stands confidently astride)* I'm like the cunning fox.

MARIAN *(sighs):* Cunning Fox, isn't it time for you to put up your sword and go to the synagogue?

PETER: Oh! It is time for school. If I'm late again, I will be in big trouble with the Rabbi.

MARIAN: And with Uncle John.

PETER *(over his shoulder):* Don't worry about me, sister. *(He exits.)*

MARIAN *(looking after him):* Oh Peter, please be careful.

*(*MARIAN, *still looking after him, pauses for three beats then turns back toward the audience, worried.* DEBORAH, JAMES, *and* TABITHA *clear props from the stage to prepare for the arrival of the* GIRLS *who will come to study the Scriptures with* MARIAN.*)*

SCENE 2

(Lights up on PETER'S *home and the* BOY'S *synagogue classroom. A simple backdrop, columns connected by draped fabric or flats painted gray with an arched window, frames the classroom scene. The only prop is the waxed slate on a wooden bench. The* BOYS *enter by twos and threes down the aisles of the auditorium to assemble in their classroom. Sitting or kneeling, they form a semicircle. At the same time,* MARIAN *welcomes the* GIRLS *who also come from the auditorium in twos and threes. They gather around* MARIAN *in a semicircle.* PETER, *wearing a fake gray beard and holding a stick, stands in front of the class and clears his throat.)*

PETER: Hrumph. Attention class.

BOY 1: Peter. If the Rabbi catches you, you will be in big trouble.

BOY 2: Peter, where's the Rabbi? Is he sick?

BOY 1: The Rabbi will pinch your ear, Peter.

PETER *(thumping stick on the floor):* Hrumph! No nonsense now. We will begin.

(Picks up a student tablet, a waxed slate, and pretends to read from it)

MARIAN: Deborah says that all of you have been studying your Scriptures. Let me see what you have learned.

ALL GIRLS: Me first! Call on me, Marian!

(Lights dim and soft music plays under this choral response. Each BOY *and* GIRL *stands to respond, then sits back down.)*

PETER: The people walking in darkness have seen a great light; on those living in the land of the shadow of death a light has dawned.

BOY 1 *(stands):* The Lord himself will give you a sign.

GIRLS: The virgin will . . . give birth to a Child and will call Him Immanuel.

ALL BOYS/GIRLS: And He will be called Wonderful, Counselor, Might God, Everlasting Father, Prince of Peace.

GIRL 1: We all, like sheep, have gone astray, each of us has turned to his own way; and the Lord has laid on Him the iniquity of us all.

BOYS: He was pierced for our transgressions, He was crushed for our iniquities; the punishment that brought us peace was upon Him, and by His wounds we are healed.

GIRL 1: He is the light of the world and the hope of all men.

BOYS: To preach good news to the poor, to bind up the broken-hearted, to proclaim freedom for the captives, to release the prisoners from darkness.

GIRLS: And of His kingdom there will be no end.

BOY 2: I will bless the Lord at all times: His praise shall continually be in my mouth.

GIRLS: O magnify the Lord with me, and let us exalt His name together.

ALL Boys / GIRLS: O taste and see that the Lord is good: blessed is the man who trusts in Him.

(All heads bow in worship as the music fades. Lights up as music ends.)

PETER: The Rabbi must not be coming today. Schools out. Yay!

BOYS: No more pens. No more scrolls. No more teachers taking roll. Yay!

(They jump, trade high fives, and chase each other out of the classroom to exit at the back of the auditorium where they will line up to reenter on the last scene. PETER, MARK, *and* TIMOTHY *exit SR and wait in the wings. The* GIRLS *in* MARIAN'S *study group say their good-byes with smiles and hugs, then exit. Lights fade on the* BOYS' *classroom.)*

SCENE 3

(Although most of the GIRLS *have left,* DORCAS, NAOMI, *and* PRISCILLA *stay behind to visit with* MARIAN.*)*

DORCAS: Marian, see my pretty new scarf? *(She turns, holding it over her head.)*

NAOMI: We thought you'd never get back.

PRISCILLA *(hands* MARIAN *a piece of colorful fabric):* It's so good to see you, Marian. I brought this for you.

MARIAN: Why, this is beautiful. Thank you, Priscilla. And thank your parents for me, also. *(Sets the fabric on the table)*

NAOMI: We would love to see your pretty silk dresses.

MARIAN: Silk dresses?

NAOMI: Yes, and your fine linens—

PRISCILLA: We know that you are in charge of all of Herod's maids, and you dress like a queen when you are in the palace.

MARIAN: Linen? Oh, girls, however did you get this idea? I'm just a maid. I clean. Well, sometimes I do a little cooking.

(These next lines are said simultaneously.)

DORCAS: Only a maid!

PRISCILLA: Oh, I'm sorry!

NAOMI: You're just a maid?

DORCAS: You're just a maid in the palace and you dress like . . . like—

(Looks at MARIAN'S *simple robe, realized the truth, and stares at her, speechless)*

PRISCILLA: Oh, Marian, we are *so* sorry. We didn't mean to hurt your feelings.

NAOMI: Deborah told us the most awesome lies about your robes and—

*(*DEBORAH, *unnoticed by the others, runs from the room.)*

DORCAS: And two maids who come when you call for one.

MARIAN: Oh, Dorcas, I'm not Herod's queen. And I'm not in charge of anything or anybody. Where is Deborah? Why would she do this?

*(*DORCAS, PRISCILLA, *and* NAOMI *look at each other, roll their eyes and shrug.* MARIAN *notices that* DEBORAH *is gone. She exits, calling for* DEBORAH. *The others follow her and exit. Three beats and* PETER, MARK, *and* TIMOTHY *enter.* PETER *limps, holds a rag over one eye, and looks disheveled, as though he has been in a fight.)*

PETER: You should have seen him, Mark. The Magi Balthazar was tall and black as ebony. He was dressed like a king—gold chains around his neck and long robes trimmed in purple. And he was on this big white horse. And there were two more kings with him.

MARK: Kings! What did *they* look like?

PETER: Oh, you should have seen them. *(Grabs* MARIAN'S *fabric, throws it over his shoulder like a cape, and brandishes his sword as he talks)* They rode horses, and they were with a huge caravan with camels, and more horses, and armed warriors, and servants! They were incredible! Anthony took one look at Balthazar and ran like a rabbit!

MARK: But why are Balthazar and those other men here?

TIMOTHY: That's the good part. They're here to find a new King, Mark! The King—our King—is here! The Messiah is in Bethlehem. We will find Him. We will no longer be slaves to Rome and to bullies like Anthony.

MARK: You can't fight Caesar's armies, Timothy. Or even one Roman soldier.

TIMOTHY: But our King is here—here in Bethlehem. With Him as our leader, we can defeat Rome. Peter and I will find Him tonight and pledge our loyalty to Him.

MARK: What do you mean? We're not men. We're no match for them. You and Peter shouldn't fight Anthony and his friends even if they do push you around. Anthony's father is a soldier.

*(*DEBORAH *enters, unnoticed.)*

PETER: And that's why he thinks he can bully us. I vow—we will find the King tonight!

MARK: Then I'll go, too.

DEBORAH: Where are you going, Peter?

(Embarrassed, PETER *pulls off his cape and dumps it in a crumpled heap on the table. He composes himself and speaks with adult dignity.)*

PETER: There are wise men from the East in town today. They say they've seen the sign of the new King of the Jews in the night sky. *They've* come to worship Him, but I will go fight for Him.

DEBORAH: Peter. Take me, too!

PETER: I won't. You're just a girl.

DEBORAH: A girl. Hah! I'm as strong as any boy. Besides, if you don't let me come, I'll tell Uncle John.

*(*MARIAN *enters. She crosses her arms and looks at* PETER.*)*

MARIAN: Tell Uncle John what?

DEBORAH: Peter is running away tonight to join the army of the new King.

MARIAN: Running away? You don't need to run away to see the new King, Peter.

PETER *(excited, takes her by the shoulders):* You have seen Him? Is He safe? Does Herod know?

MARIAN: Yes, I have seen Him. And I . . . I hope Herod doesn't know.

PETER *(disbelieving):* How do you know this when no one else does!

MARIAN: But many *do* know. You remember when the Emperor made everyone go back to their hometowns for the census? I helped Aunt Lydia feed guests at the inn. A very strange thing happened. One night, some shepherds came to the inn where we were working. They said that angels sent them to see the King. And they weren't talking about Herod.

PETER *(pacing excitedly):* Angels? Yes, yes, of course. And He *was* there? And you didn't tell us!

MARIAN: Yes—

TIMOTHY: The inn? Can we see Him?

MARIAN *(thoughtful):* Shepherds were allowed to see Him, so surely it would be all right for us to visit. But that was months ago. I heard He's staying somewhere else now.

MARK: Can we go now? Today?

MARIAN: I need to feed the children first, but yes, we can go today.

*(*MARIAN *takes* DEBORAH *aside, out of the hearing of the* BOYS, *who mime excited conversation among themselves.)*

MARIAN: Deborah, why did you run away this afternoon?

DEBORAH: Oh, Marian, nobody loves me, and I . . . I've been bad. And I'm tired of being poor. I don't have pretty dresses like Dorcas or nice things like Naomi.

MARIAN: You *are loved*, Deborah, but sometimes you won't let us show it. Come, let's get the children. We will all go to see the new King as soon as we've had our evening meal.

*(*MARIAN *exits with her arm around* DEBORAH'S *shoulder.)*

PETER *(to his friends):* Men! Bring your weapons, but conceal them.

(The next lines are said simultaneously.)

MARK: We will be ready.

TIMOTHY: I'm ready, Peter!

*(*PETER, MARK, TIMOTHY, MARIAN, *and* DEBORAH *exit to join the rest of the cast at the back of the auditorium. All* CHILDREN *prepare to reenter carrying lamps or battery-operated candles.)*

SCENE 4

(Blackout on the stage and in the auditorium. The auditorium aisles are the paths that the CHILDREN *travel to see the child. As the* CHILDREN *enter from the back of the auditorium carrying lanterns or batter-operated candles, soft music begins and underscores the scene. The older* CHILDREN *hold the hands of the very young.)*

MIRIAM: Watch your step. The street is bad on this side of town.

PETER: Is He here with His army?

CHILD 1: Will He see us?

CHILD 2: Carry me. I'm tired.

TABITHA: I want Aunt Lydia. I want to go home!

PETER *(fuming):* This is men's work. You shouldn't have brought the children, Marian.

MARIAN: Oh, Peter, we couldn't leave them. When they're grown, they will remember this night and tell their children about it.

PETER: Well, I don't like it!

(They stop just before they reach the wooden house where JOSEPH *stands beside* MARY. *Seated on the wooden chair or bench, she holds* JESUS *in her arms.)*

MARIAN: Here we are.

PETER: A King stays here? Where would He quarter His men?

DEBORAH: This is not a palace!

MARIAN: Deborah, Peter, hush.

(Lights are brought up until the scene is lit softly. CHILDREN *split into two groups, one led by* MARIAN, *the other by* PETER. CHILDREN *gather about* JESUS, *but do not block the audience view. Their eyes are wide with amazement and delight.)*

MARIAN: Mary, we've come to see your Child—if it's all right with you.

JOSEPH *(smiles at* MARY, *then* MARIAN*):* Welcome.

CHILD 1: Where is His horse?

CHILD 2: Where is His king-crown?

CHILD 1: He's a baby!

CHILD 2: He has little fingers.

(All CHILDREN *talk quietly among themselves, oohing and ahhing, and making comments: He's precious. He's sweet. Isn't He cute?)*

MARIAN: Jesus, I would like You to meet my brother Peter and his friends. We are here to pledge to You our loyalty and our love. *(She puts her arm around* DEBORAH.*)* He was born in a stable, Deborah.

DEBORAH: But He's our King! Our Savior! He could have been born in a palace! *(She reaches out to take His hand.)* Look, He likes me! He won't let go of my fingers. Does that mean He likes me? Do you think God will forgive me for lying, Marian?

MARIAN: When we are truly sorry and ask Him to forgive us, He does, Deborah.

PETER: Well, I thought He'd be older than me. He . . . He would get hurt on a sword. What can I give Him?

MARIAN: What you came to give Him—your allegiance and your love.

(Music swells)

PETER *(kneels and places the sword at* JESUS' *feet):* My King!

(All CHILDREN *bow their heads to signal the end of the drama, then close in song as they are gathered around* JESUS.*)*